The Walk Around Santa Cruz Book

The Walk Around Santa Cruz Book
A Look at the City's Architectural Treasures

by Margaret Koch

595519

FRESNO **Valley Publishers** 1978

Valley Publishers
8 East Olive Avenue
Fresno, California 93728

Library of Congress Catalog Number 78-65265
ISBN 0-913548-61-8

Mission Hill Area

Mission Hill was where the city of Santa Cruz got its start as the twelfth of the 21 Alta California Missions founded by the Franciscan padres.

The first hotel, the Eagle, and the first business establishments in the mission settlement were located in adobe structures which were clustered around the Mission Plaza. In those days the Plaza served as Indian gathering place to receive food rations, as a place to tie horses, or to butcher a cow for the mission meat supply.

Today, of the many adobes in the mission compound, only the School Street Adobe remains. To see it you will walk on one of the city's first paved sidewalks (blacktop mined in the county).

Holy Cross Church, designed by Thomas J. Welch, was built in 1889. Noteworthy are its painted ceiling panels, and, out in front, the Gothic-style granite arch placed in 1891 as a memorial.

Mission Hill Area

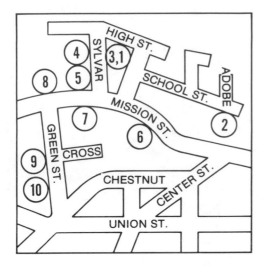

The first five listed are all located around Holy Cross Plaza within one short block. Proceed to Mission Street, turn left to see Leslie Building which sits on brow of hill. Then retrace steps to proceed along Mission past Halsey House and Gingerbread House to Green Street. Turn left down Green Street for Houses No. 9 and 10.

(1) Santa Cruz Mission—Emmett and High Streets. This is a replica of the mission originally built in the 1790s.

(2) School Street Adobe—130 School Street. This is the only surviving structure of the original mission compound.

(3) Holy Cross Church—126 High Street. This English Gothic church, built in 1889, has a 149-foot spire.

(4) Alzina House—109 Sylvar Street. The home of Santa Cruz county's first sheriff, this house is almost 130 years old.

(5) The Willey House—105 Sylvar Street. This lovely home features several stained glass windows.

(6) Leslie Brick Building—155 Mission Street. The secret of this building is well-hidden beneath many coats of plaster.

(7) Halsey House—207 Mission Street. This imposing structure is one of the finest examples extant of Eastlake style.

(8) Gingerbread House—218 Mission Street. Built in 1867, this house and its twin next door both have a fairy tale charm.

(9) Alice's House—127 Green Street. This house is an interesting combination of Victorian Gothic and Greek Revival.

(10) Sadler House—123 Green Street. Inside this handsome house hides a tiny wooden building which was once a church.

– 1931 –
Santa Cruz Mission
Emmett and High Streets

This replica of the original mission was built in 1931-32 and follows the design faithfully, though it is about half as large as the original.

When the Franciscan padres first came here to establish what was to be the twelfth in the chain of missions, they put up a rude shelter of wood slats stuck into the ground, probably with a thatched roof, "down in the flat." The exact site is not known. They soon moved up onto Mission Hill, where they built the full-fledged mission, safe from the flooding San Lorenzo River.

The mission was composed of stone and adobe, its 25-foot high walls built of stone to the height of three feet and then adobe to the eaves. It was 112 feet long and 30 feet wide, and was topped first with thatch, then later with tiles.

This mission had everything in its favor: rich crop lands, a fine water supply, stone and lumber resources, and Indians to do the work. An orchard was put in, grain fields and vegetable crops were planted; a water-powered grist mill was installed; adjoining adobe buildings were put up to house soldiers, weaving looms, blacksmith shop, storerooms, leather-working, offices, priests' quarters, and a guardhouse. By 1797 there were 644 souls counted as saved.

But that same year Villa de Branciforte, a civil settlement, was established just across the river. It was an easy-going place which offered many pleasures that soon became more popular with the Indian neophytes than work and church. By 1800 the Indian population was down to 492 due to disease, death, and desertion.

In 1812 one of the priests was murdered. In 1818 the threat of a French pirate, de Bouchard, to sack the mission panicked the priests and they turned the mission over to Villa officials and fled over the mountains with their neophytes. Rough weather at sea kept the pirate from landing, but when the priests returned they discovered that the Villa officials had guarded the mission so well that much of it had disappeared forever—including barrels of wine and other supplies.

The secularization of the missions in 1834-35 was the final blow. Mission properties valued at $50,000 seemed to evaporate into thin air and eventually the mission buildings fell into crumbling ruins, helped along by heavy rain storms and earthquakes. The last vestiges were demolished in 1889.

– c. 1800 –
School Street Adobe
136 School Street

The only remaining original adobe of the Santa Cruz Mission compound was also the first duplex in the city. It is actually two separate living quarters separated by a five-foot-thick adobe wall. Its first function and exact age are unknown, but the mission was built in 1793-94, so it is possible that this building was erected as early as 1796. A plaque says it was built in 1810. At any rate, it is very old!

It is known that the mission compound originally included a school, sleeping quarters for Indian women, and a guardhouse. This building is believed by many to have been the guardhouse.

When the mission was secularized and turned over to civil authorities in 1834-35, some of the church property, including this adobe, was divided among the few remaining Costanoan Indians. In 1838 Jose de la Rodriguez paid the Indians two cows and two mules for one half of the adobe. The other half was sold to Patrick Neary in 1865.

The Rodriguez and Neary families retained their respective portions and made them their homes until 1957, when the State of California purchased the historic building for a State Historical Landmark. Miss Alice Neary sold her half outright and it housed an antique shop until recently. Mrs. Cornelia Hopcroft, a Rodriguez heir, retained a life tenancy and still makes her home in her half of the adobe.

In 1965 when rains threatened to melt a portion of the adobe, the State Division of Beaches and Parks reroofed the building. When the old roof was removed, evidence was uncovered that indicates it was originally a one-story adobe instead of two—another mystery about the origin of this relic of yesterday.

– 1889 –
Holy Cross Church
126 High Street

On August 28, 1791, a cross was raised to mark the site of what was to become the twelfth of the Alta California Missions and the foundation of the city of Santa Cruz, Mission Santa Cruz, or more formally, La Exaltacion de la Santa Cruz.

With the passing of years and the collapse of the mission system, Mission Santa Cruz became Holy Cross Church.

The first wood church building, built to replace the ruined adobe Mission sanctuary, had twin towers and was dedicated July 4, 1858. It served until 1889 when the present brick church building was completed.

The English Gothic Holy Cross Church of today was designed by Thomas J. Welsh, San Francisco architect. Its tall spire rises 149 feet. Of special note: the Gothic memorial arch in front of the church, put up in 1891.

– c. 1850 –
Alzina House
109 Sylvar Street

This is the oldest wood frame house in Santa Cruz, built circa 1850. A fireplace and chimney which were added later were recently removed to restore authenticity.

Francisco Alzina was the first Sheriff of the newly-created Santa Cruz County, serving from 1850 to 1858. He and his wife, the former Maria Gonzales, built their little house at the corner of Mission and Sylvar, where the Willey House is. The Alzina's house was moved over when the Willey's house was built.

It has always been said that the lumber for the Alzina house was hauled down the coast from Maria's father's Rancho Pescadero. Francisco and Maria lived out their lives in this house, raising 14 children. Maria outlived her husband by a good number of years. As long as she lived, she could be seen every morning, dressed in dark skirts with a black shawl over her head, crossing the Plaza to go to mass in Holy Cross Church. One son, Enoch, was a deputy sheriff of Santa Cruz County and made his home with his mother.

– 1893 –
Willey House
105 Sylvar Street

Built in 1887, Willey House is late Eastlake with several fine stained glass windows. Notable are the porch railings, the brackets and ornamental box beneath the window over the main entry. Brackets also adorn the underside of the second story porch, which is supported on slender columns. The house is finished in smooth siding with one side band of ornamental shingles under the eaves.

Henry Willey used redwood from Santa Cruz County forests to build his home. The floors of the main rooms are parquet hardwood, but redwood was also used for ornate paneling in the living and dining rooms, and for the big sliding doors that separate them. A small conservatory opened off the south porch and the dining room.

The house was built at a cost of $5,000 for Willey's bride, a young widow named Mary Weldon Sinnott who was known as "Mrs. Molly" after her marriage to Willey. They lived happily in their large house for four years. Then Mrs. Molly and their infant son died in childbirth. For seven years Henry was a lonely widower—and then he met a blue-eyed music teacher, Frances Lockhart. In 1898 "Miss Fanny" became the new Mrs. Henry Willey and brought life back into the big house on the hill. The Willeys lived there until 1926.

Mrs. George W. Cooper, the next owner, rented the house to Mrs. Helen Mowry, who operated a lampshade factory there for a few years. In 1943 Mrs. Cooper sold the house to the Daughters (Sisters) of Charity, with the sale price between $2,000 and $3,000—almost unbelievable. In 1954 the house was sold to Robert Dodt, who sold it to Mrs. Gwendolyn Niemeyer, who sold it to Mitch Keil in 1973. It has changed hands several times since.

– c. 1850 –
Leslie Brick Building
155 Mission Street

Most passersby would not look twice, maybe not even once, at this building. If they did look, their thought might be: It's a poor imitation of a Mission Revival style.

Not so. Underneath its many coats of plaster exists the first brick building to be constructed in Santa Cruz. This fact is barely known today.

Nothing is known of the man named Leslie who built the structure at the top of Mission Hill. Even the year of its construction is a mystery, but in the late Ernest Otto's writings there are several mentions of this building as "the first brick building in Santa Cruz."

A fair guess would be 1850, because by 1852 the city's center of business was moving down onto "the flat," where it is today.

Leslie, whoever he was, apparently did not remain long in Santa Cruz. The brick building was constructed with living quarters upstairs, a common plan in that era. Originally it had plain rectangular windows with dark iron shutters. It was built of the soft red brick that was manufactured in one of several brick yards in Santa Cruz.

When Mission Hill School was located next door, the building served as a neighborhood grocery (and penny candy shop), with living quarters still upstairs.

– 1883 –
Halsey House
207 Mission Street

Probably the finest example of Eastlake style still standing in Santa Cruz, Halsey House was built in 1883. Its original carriage house is still out back. Fireplaces are French Towle work, handpainted with turkey feathers to simulate marble. Locks, hinges and knobs downstairs are all the original brass. Doors have "woodgraining," a Victorian fad wherein paint and varnish were mixed and applied to paneling to simulate wood grain. The wallpaper border in the front parlor and the painted ceilings in the parlor and dining room are the originals. Floors are redwood, with fir or pine in the kitchen. The ceiling panels containing the popular Victorian stork have been restored. The upstairs bath still has its tub on legs, but the kitchen and the downstairs bath have been modernized.

For years this house has stood, tall and commanding. Its imposing facade seems to demand that all eyes turn to it as they pass by on Mission Street. The owners and occupants of the house for many years were the Halsey sisters, both schoolteachers. Miss Alice Halsey taught in Santa Cruz schools for more than 40 years, retiring in 1938. Her sister, Clara, was in Santa Cruz a shorter time, as she had married George Taylor, lived in Mountain View, and produced a son before she was widowed. The sisters lived quietly, dressed somberly, and taught the three R's without nonsense. They both died in 1961.

– 1867 –
Gingerbread House
218 Mission Street

Gingerbread House has had the good fortune to pass through the hands of several young couples who loved old houses and treated them to tender loving care—most recently the Dave Brockmanns.

Rewiring, replacing modern woodwork with old, modern moldings with the old-fashioned kind, and new wallpaper with authentic old patterns—those are the kinds of things that have been done to the little house. There is a modern addition on the rear, but it hardly shows and certainly does not detract from the front appearance, which is one of fairy tale charm.

Gingerbread and its twin next door were built side by side on 44-foot lots by Louis Schwartz, who also built a third house, much larger, for himself, just a step away. He rented out the two smaller houses.

The houses were built in 1867. Note the stickwork and the ornate porch railings of Gingerbread House. Its slender turned pillars hold the second story porch with gentle arches between them. The narrow little house is sided with clapboard shiplap of redwood from Santa Cruz County lumber mills.

Louis Schwartz climbed the ladder of success rung by rung, from the time he left his native Prussia to learn the baking trade, through a period in England and another in New York, and finally in California. He crossed the Isthmus of Panama and floated into San Francisco Harbor on the *Uncle Sam* in 1854 with exactly $7 in his pocket. A year later, in partnership, he opened a merchandise store in Santa Cruz which prospered and gave rise to branch stores in San Luis Obispo, Santa Maria and Cayucos, as well as lumber yards. He also had interests in a fleet of cargo ships.

In 1865 Schwartz married Miss Rebecca Stein. they were the parents of eight children, four of whom survived to adulthood.

Gingerbread's twin at 214 Mission Street is the home of Carmen Guichard, a member of another pioneer family. Carmen still uses a little wood stove for heat and raises almost all of her vegetables in the backyard.

– c. 1869 –
Alice's House
127 Green Street

The basic form of Alice's House is Victorian Gothic Revival, but the entrance, the windows, and the balanced symmetry of the house point to Greek Revival. It was built before 1870, probably by Otis A. Longley.

The "Alice" was Alice Edith Farnham, only child of Enoch George Farnham, who bought the house and property from Silas Randall in 1878. Alice left her mark on the house: scratched into one of the old bubble-glass windows are the initials A.E.F. She also planted the huge Belle of Portugal rose bush at the corner of the front porch.

The residents of Green Street, where Alice's House stands, feel that they have something special—it is the kind of street that contributes to Santa Cruz's charm and unique "New England" atmosphere. In the early days Green Street was the main thoroughfare that led up and over Mission Hill, connecting the downtown "flat" with the Potrero north of it on present-day River Street. Instead of the extension of North Pacific which skirts the chalk rock bluff of Mission Hill, a waterfall cascaded over that same bluff to form a pool at its base, from which it flowed into the San Lorenzo River.

Green Street was named for a man who donated lumber for the first Methodist Church building which was located on the southeast corner of Green and Mission Streets, but which of the several men named Green was that one seems uncertain. A John D. Green came to Santa Cruz in 1847, married Lydia Hitchcock, and bought "Crazy" Wright's sawmill in 1849 for $2,000. The sawmill was located at Rincon, up the San Lorenzo canyon, and is said to have furnished lumber for the First Methodist Church, so chances are good that Green Street was named for that Mr. Green. But there was also an E. G. Green whose wife was active in the WCTU, and a J. S. Green who lived in Washington Street. In fact there were so many Greens in early-day California that a noted historian threw up his hands, figuratively speaking, and gave up trying to get them all straight.

– 1850 –
Sadler House
123 Green Street

To look at this handsome old house today, one would never suspect its humble beginnings.

Up the street from it, on the southeast corner of Green and Mission Streets, the Methodists constructed their first church, a plain wood building 30 by 20 feet, in 1850. It served until 1864 when a new sanctuary was built.

Eager to pay off their $4,000 debt on the new building, church trustees decided to sell part of the church property of seven acres. They sold a row of lots along what became the west side of Green Street to a young man named Otis Longley who had just acquired a bride. He in turn sold part of the land to William J. Reynolds, who paid Otis $125 for a lot, then bargained with the church fathers for the discarded "box" church building. He moved it down Green Street to his lot and added rooms to it. Three years later he sold the house and land for $6,000 to James Dougherty, a Santa Clara Valley lumberman.

There were several other owners over the years— T. W. Kelly, D. C. Clark (superintendent of the city's schools), and Mrs. Don Sadler, Clark's daughter. Mr. and Mrs. Edward Tunheim acquired it in 1964 and cherish it greatly. Mr. Tunheim has gone underneath the house and established the location of its oldest portion, the Methodist "box." Over 125 years old, it is still sound, its virgin redwood intact.

Pacific Garden Mall
(Pacific Avenue)

When one raises one's eyes to the rooftops while walking along Pacific Garden Mall, formerly Pacific Avenue, interesting architectural details are visible. The usual busy shopper rarely looks up to catch sight of the early names and dates, the handsome cornices and pediments which still adorn some of the older buildings.

Pacific Avenue, Front Street, and the heart of Santa Cruz rest on some of the richest river-laid land in the county. The Franciscan Padres of Mission Santa Cruz were canny agriculturalists. They planted the "flat" to vegetables which they sold to visiting sailing ships. Pacific Avenue was then a row of willow trees along an irrigation ditch. The street was first named Willow Street, then was changed to Pacific Avenue in the 1860s when the trees were cut down.

The early businesses which had been clustered around the Mission Plaza up on the hill, began to move down to the flat in the 1850s. Front Street was named "Main Street" and was the main business thoroughfare with the early-day hotel, the Santa Cruz House, and Goodwin and Martin's Livery Stable located where today the Veterans Building stands.

First grocery store on the flat was that of Charles Eldon, located at the southwest corner of the junction of Mission, Pacific and Water Streets. Today the restored and renovated Town Clock sits on the site of

Elihu Anthony's pioneer iron foundry and shop where he turned out picks for gold miners.

The pie-shaped building at the juncture of Front and Pacific is known as the Flatiron Building, constructed of locally-made bricks about 1860.

Across Pacific Avenue was Williamson and Garrett's Grocery Store—the name is still there high under the eaves. Walking south on Pacific one passes the St. George Hotel at Number 1520, a Spanish Colonial design on this side, and its original Victorian facade on its Front Street side. The hotel was built for A. P. Hotaling of San Francisco in 1894-95. In its day it was elegant, with a glass-roofed garden court containing a fountain and fern garden. The Spanish plaster re-modeling on the front facade was done in 1922.

Proceeding south, turn the corner onto Cooper Street to see Cooper House, which is the former County Court House, and the Octagon Museum, which is the former Hall of Records.

Again, raise your eyes to the upper reaches of the Leonard Building at the corner of Cooper and Front. built in 1894. The upper floor yet retains the round corner by and the grapevine motif designed for it by architect Edward Van Cleeck—one of downtown Santa Cruz's unexpected architectural gems.

Pacific Garden Mall

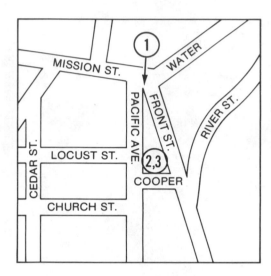

Start at the reconstructed Town Clock (restoration begun in 1974). Bullet holes in Flatiron are now plastered over. Proceed south on Pacific Garden Mall, observing old names, dates, pediments and decorations on many of the older commercial buildings. Then go from the Museum north on Front Street to observe original rear facade of St. George Hotel.

1. **Flatiron Building—Pacific and Front Streets.** The first brick building erected "down on the flat," this 120-year-old structure has been recommended for Historical Landmark status.
2. **Cooper House—110 Cooper Street.** Once the county courthouse, this impressive building now houses boutique shops and a restaurant and bar.
3. **Octagon Museum—Cooper and Front Streets.** Saved from demolition ten years ago, this unique brick building is now the County Museum.

– 1859 –
Flatiron Building
Pacific Avenue and Front Street

Hugo Hihn, brother of Frederick A. Hihn, had the Flatiron Building constructed in 1859-60, of bricks made right in Santa Cruz.

It was the first brick building to be erected "down on the flat," as most of the business structures formerly had been up on the Mission Santa Cruz Plaza.

The curiously shaped building, which looks like a piece of pie blunted on the point, served as the Santa Cruz County Courthouse for a time, later as a drugstore, and today as a Chinese Restaurant upstairs and a bakery downstairs.

The wildest tale regarding this old building was the one beloved by small boys who would show visitors where "the bullet fired at the bandit Tiburcio Vasquez made a hole in the Flatiron Building."

Today this is one of 18 structures in Santa Cruz City which have been recommended for Historical Landmark status.

– 1894 –
Cooper House
110 Cooper Street

Built in 1894-95, Cooper House was designed by Comstock and constructed by Thomas Beck at a cost of $53,475. It was Santa Cruz County's fifth courthouse. A Richardson Romanesque Revival building, it is said to be one of only two or three of its kind west of the Mississippi. When it was built it was considered very advanced for a town the size of Santa Cruz.

It is constructed of sand mold "gold" bricks, with brownstone brick facing. Of particular note are the arched brick ceilings of the basement. Its graceful double staircase had been long closed up and unused by the county, but was opened and restored to use by Max Walden, the present owner. The carved rail was duplicated, as was the original iron work.

The very first courthouse business in Santa Cruz County was conducted in the Eagle Hotel on the Mission Plaza. After a couple of years the county bought Thomas Fallon's combination home and store, also on the upper Plaza, for $3,500. By 1860, when it was becoming obvious that the main business of the town was all down on the flat (where it is today), the county moved its headquarters into the second floor of the brick Flatiron Building. In 1867 the Cooper brothers, William and John, gave land for the county's first "real" Courthouse, that is, a building built for that purpose. It was a brick building and cost the unbelievable sum of $20,000. After it burned in the great fire of April 14, 1894, the second Courthouse, the building now known as Cooper House, was built on the same site.

The building was in danger of demolition for a while, after the county moved out in 1967. But Max Walden bought it and transformed it. There are now boutique shops and a bar on the first and second floors and a restaurant and liquor store in the basement. There is also an outdoor sidewalk cafe in good weather, with a music combo playing for the enjoyment of all.

–c. 1882–
Octagon Museum
Cooper and Front Streets

On March 11, 1882, the Santa Cruz County Board of Supervisors began advertising for plans for a "Hall of Records" building. On April 8 of the same year, drawings and specifications for an octagonal brick building were presented to the Board. The shape was said to have been taken from a $50 octagonal-shaped gold piece minted in San Francisco in 1851-52.

The cornerstone-laying took place on June 10, 1882, with Santa Cruz Masonic Lodge officiating and Governor George C. Perkins of California as the main guest of honor. Wood seats were hastily built to accommodate the crowds. The ceremony was followed by a dance with a five-piece orchestra playing such tunes as "Darling Nelly Gray" and "Listen to the Mocking Bird."

On October 7, 1882, the finished octagon was turned over to the county and a warrant was drawn to pay for it. The unique building served Santa Cruz County as its Hall of Records for 86 years, although the last two or three decades were punctuated with cries for "more room." In the early 1920s an ugly brick appendage was added to the Front Street side in a attempt to provide needed space.

When the County began to build a new Governmental Center for itself, people who had passed the old octagon for years without really seeing it began to take a second look. The building's rarity and architectural importance had been taken for granted for years.

When demolition rumors began to fly about, a few people began to work for its preservation. The rumors even reached the historically tuned ears of Donald C. Biggs, director of the California Historical Society at that time. He had led the battle to save Portsmouth Plaza and the San Francisco Mint, and he was just as concerned about the impending loss of Santa Cruz's octagon.

In February 1968 the County Board of Supervisors passed a resolution preserving the brick octagon as a County Museum. With the aid of a historic preservation grant from HUD (U.S. Department of Housing and Urban Development), the restoration was carried out and the museum was dedicated on June 17, 1972.

Downtown Residential Area

The downtown residential district of Santa Cruz was divided into several areas in early days when houses became more numerous than farms and pastures.

The Walnut Avenue, Church Street and Locust Street area contained the most sought-after addresses by the stylish families. South of Walnut Avenue the parallel streets of Lincoln and Laurel enclosed more modest dwellings. And still further south, beyond Laurel, at one time there was located Santa Cruz's Chinatown (a settlement which found it expedient to move three or four times during its life span.)

The downtown residential area south of Walnut Avenue in recent years (1910s through 1950s) had fallen upon unfavorable times. Many houses were rundown; in a city famed for its flower gardens yards were weedy and neglected; property values sagged along with the shabbier frame dwellings.

All this has been changed in the past 16 years—but not without the almost magical foresight, unshakeable faith and tremendous effort on the part of many people. At the fore, prodding, pushing, cajoling, arguing gently but urgently, smiling and lecturing, was the late Chuck Abbott, who finally won over his audiences who were hard-headed businessmen.

Chuck convinced them that downtown Santa Cruz did not have to die on the vine as it appeared to be doing. He is best remembered as the "Father of Pacific Garden Mall." But it was Chuck who first recognized the potential of the rundown residential area adjoining Pacific Avenue, and who established his own home there to show what could be done with a house that was just plain "old."

Today, PROD continues the work Chuck Abbott began, and modest little Victorians are beginning to bloom again where weeds flourished just a few years ago.

Downtown Residential Area

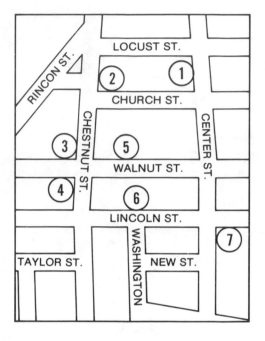

Start at City Hall and go west on Church Street to Chestnut Street. Houses No. 3 and 4 are on Chestnut. Then turn east on Walnut Avenue to see No. 5. Return to Chestnut and proceed south one block to Lincoln to see PROD developments in area which includes Washington Street. Then go one block down Lincoln to Center Street to see No. 7.

1. **Santa Cruz City Hall—Center and Church Streets.** The 1937 structure is Monterey Colonial; an addition was built in 1965.
2. **Heiner-Bowen House—346 Church Street.** Built in 1877, this structure is now used as offices for City Parks and Recreation.
3. **Haslam House—304 Walnut Street.** In the last 10 years, this elaborate home has been restored to its full Victorian splendor.
4. **Santa Cruz YWCA—303 Walnut Street.** A departure from the usual Santa Cruz architecture, this has its own attractive style.
5. **Triplett House—240 Walnut Street.** Small but elegant, this Queen Anne house is almost a century old.
6. **PROD—406 Lincoln Street.** There is a fascinating story to these well-kept flats.
7. **Calvary Episcopal Church—532 Center Street.** This is a beautiful building with an interesting history.

– 1937 –
City Hall
Center at Church

When Santa Cruz began to outgrow the old Hihn mansion, which had served as its City Hall from 1923 to 1937, the city fathers began to think about a new City Hall on the same site. Plans were drawn up by C. J. Ryland for a new building to be built in three sections: a northerly wing on Locust Street, a central section, and a south wing on Church Street. It was to be one-story, with a porch around the U-shaped courtyard for which a fountain was planned. The structure is Monterey Colonial in architectural style.

The old mansion was demolished to make way for the new City Hall, which served well for nearly 30 years. Then in 1965, once again faced with the problem of adequate space for its growing departments, the City of Santa Cruz had plans drawn for an addition to the City Hall. Robert Stevens Associates designed a two-story structure which was placed to the west of the existing building. Architecturally it is a pleasing and well-designed part of the whole.

In 1937, the cost of the new City Hall was $144,857, of which the Federal Government paid about $60,000 and the Santa Cruz Rifle Club paid $140. The Spanish gardens, which are universally admired and commented on, initially cost $9,000. The recent addition cost $300,000 and added 10,000 square feet of space.

There are two fountains splashing and bright flowers blooming almost all the year 'round, at Santa Cruz City Hall.

– 1877 –
Heiner-Bowen House
346 Church Street

Stick style with touches of Eastlake and, in its fish-scale shingles, a reminder of Queen Anne, this is a fascinating old structure. It was purchased by the City of Santa Cruz in 1970, restored and remodeled, and is in use as offices for the Department of City Parks and Recreation.

One of the city's first duplexes, this house was built in 1877 for Mrs. Rosanna Bowen by two carpenters named Alexander and Marsh. Their original estimate was $2,000, but the final cost was $1,373. It contained ten rooms, was two stories high, and boasted closets. The site was the former location of the E. Kunitz Soap and Glue Factory, which had been moved out to River Street.

H. O. Heiner acquired the building in about 1926. He planted the redwood tree, now 100 feet tall, to the west of the house. Each summer the tree is almost completely covered with a mass of Bougainvillea blossoms from a vine which climbs to its top. Heiner and his wife, Inez, were known for their interest in animals and were instrumental in the establishment of the S.P.C.A. facility at Delaveaga Park.

The city's remodeling and rehabilitating project involved a complete rewiring job, installation of baseboard electric heat, and some slight remodeling of the bathrooms. Most of the work was done by Parks and Recreation personnel, and the total cost was only $15,000. There is the main downstairs office, conference room, lavatories and small kitchen, and upstairs are four offices, bath, and storage.

– 1893 –
Haslam House
304 Walnut Avenue

Framed by large trees, one of them the "monkey tree" that was so popular in Santa Cruz around the turn of the century, a pale green Queen Anne house rises to a majestic height at the corner of Walnut Avenue and Chestnut Street. It has many elaborate "fishscale" shingles; the boxed cornices are frieze decorated; and the tower has a finial.

The house was designed by architect E. L. Van Cleek and built by contractor J. B. Dawson, at a cost of $4,500, in 1893. It was on one of the most stylish streets in town. However, its location served another purpose, too: its owner could walk to work from there, and did.

Built of local redwood, the house has a parlor, living room, dining room, entry hall, office, three bedrooms on the second floor, and baths, and a full attic and handsome oak staircase. In recent years, while being used as an antique shop, the front porch was closed in with glass panels. Only the kitchen and baths have been modernized, and in the last 10 years the house has been restored to its full Victorian splendor.

The original owner of the house, William D. Haslam, was born in Santa Cruz in 1860. In 1877 his father died and the young man found himself with his mother and sister to support. He displayed great business acumen and achieved success at a young age; he was only 33 when he built this lovely home for himself.

– 1921 –
Y.W.C.A.
303 Walnut Avenue

The main YWCA building in Santa Cruz looks as if it should be located in some European town, rather than rubbing elbows with the Victorians which surround it on three sides. When the Salvator Fachutars built it as their studio-home in 1921-22, they ignored past and present Santa Cruz architectural trends and chose a plain two-story box-like structure with hip roof and small-paned windows. They also placed it almost on the sidewalks of two sides, and had a wire fence constructed between it and passers-by. It's a curious building, attractive in an unusual way, perhaps for its purity of line.

Mr. Fachutar was a perfume chemist and this house was a perfume factory. He was also a violin-maker and composer, and the building was said to be the "largest music house between San Francisco and Los Angeles, and the only one in Santa Cruz handling all sheet music and musical literature in addition to all varieties of perfumes and lovely perfume bottles."

After Mr. Fachutar died in 1939, his widow continued to live on in the studio-home. Frances Bagnell Fachutar was something of a celebrity in her own right. She carried on her husband's projects of helping young musicians financially.

In 1944, Mrs. Fachutar, in failing health, sold her home and property to the Santa Cruz YWCA, which had been a part of the Monterey YWCA District until 1942. With the home, the eager Y women got the large garden in which grew the roses and other flowers from which Mr. Fachutar had distilled his perfumes.

For years the YWCA was housed comfortably in the structure, but recently acquired the combination Eastlake and Queen Anne house next door at 315 Walnut Avenue, to help ease growing pains.

– c. 1878 –
Triplett House
240 Walnut Avenue

This small architectural jewel is about 100 years old, and was built, along with its twin next door, by W. A. Reese, according to an old building record. Over the years, the street number changed from 96 Walnut Avenue to 98, then finally to 240 Walnut Avenue. In the days when Victorian society was at its pompous height in Santa Cruz, Walnut Avenue was *the* address to have.

This house has seven rooms, a small tower, curving front porch, fancy shingles and spindles, and is Queen Anne style.

For more than 30 years, every woman in Santa Cruz County who went into Leask's Department Store in Santa Cruz for gloves or ribbons was acquainted with Anita Triplett. Ladies wore gloves—and ribbons—in those days. Anita, a frail little old maid, would have them rest their elbows on a small velvet cushion on the counter top, then would gently, so gently, ease the tight new gloves onto their fingers one by one, and down over their hands.

Nita, as she was always called, was one of four Triplett sisters. They had fine old Spanish blood in their veins, but they seldom, if ever, mentioned it. Their grandparents were Simon and Petra Perez, who were married in 1849 at Santa Cruz Mission. They owned much of the area at the eastern edge of Santa Cruz and the land where Dominican Hospital is located today. There were ten children, including Josephine, who married Remus Triplett and had four daughters: Anita, Pearl, Josephine and Mabel.

Josephine married, but Mabel, Anita and Pearl remained maiden ladies who were devout members of Holy Cross Church and led quiet lives; only Anita ventured into the business world. They bought the elegant little house on Walnut Avenue in 1945, and it was their home until they died, one by one. Pearl lived the longest, and before she died she burned old pictures and documents, the thought of which is enough to make a historian weep.

PROD
(Private Revitalization of Downtown)

The late Chuck Abbott and his wife, Esther, both nationally-known photographers, came to Santa Cruz to retire in 1963. They planned to take it easy, except for their fall and spring auto trips to photograph scenery for national magazines.

Instead of taking it easy, they found several major projects that needed "doing" in Santa Cruz. First there was Pacific Avenue to do something about. Chuck decided a mall was the answer to the dying downtown, and eventually Pacific Garden Mall became a reality.

But the mall wasn't enough. Chuck and Esther purchased several older houses, refurbished and restored them, lived in one and rented out the others.

These weren't big fancy Victorians. They were the ordinary kind of house that average families occupied around the turn of the century. In "recycling" the older, less desirable houses, the Abbotts actually started a "recycling" wave in their neighborhood, with near neighbors painting and fixing up and planting street trees. Their block on Lincoln Street took on a more pleasant aura. But just a few doors away, on the same street, there were rundown houses that challenged Chuck. In fact there was a whole row of look-alike flats with peeling paint, sagging porches, and postage-stamp front yards filled with thriving weeds.

These flats had once been handsome, and Chuck felt they could be again. After months of work, planning, and negotiations, PROD (Private Revitalization of Downtown) was born. The Abbotts acquired the row of flats and put a crew of eager college students to work in their spare time. Tons of trash were removed, porches were repaired, interiors were renovated, painted, re-wired. The flats were painted a soft green with brick trim and the tiny front yards were paved with used bricks and planted with trees and ivy. The flats were rented to students who raise their own vegetables in the large backyard which runs through the center of the block.

It is easy to take a stately Victorian and do something spectacular with it. It's not easy to take run-down, ordinary old houses and make them into something attractive that can be rented at average rental prices to average people. Not everyone can live in a mansion. It's also not an easy project to upgrade less desirable neighborhoods, but Chuck and Esther Abbott showed how it can be done in an economically feasible way.

– 1864 –
Calvary Episcopal Church
538 Center Street

This wood Victorian Gothic Revival building has been acclaimed an "architectural jewel." It was built in 1864 for approximately $4,000, from plans drawn by Joseph Boston, who, it is said, designed his church after one in England. Of special note is the beautiful curved apse with its six stained glass windows. It is the oldest known church building in continuous use in California. It is also the first church in the state and the first building in Santa Cruz to receive a bronze plaque from the California Heritage Council. James W. Lenhoff, president of the Council, presented the plaque on June 16, 1972.

At the center of the beginning of Calvary Episcopal Church was a frail girl who had come to California from New York in search of health.

Eliza Bull arrived in California in 1861 and found health and a husband and family. She founded the church in Santa Cruz, became the mother of five children, and was the first local woman to serve as a public school trustee. She was a writer and a much-sought speaker. She also was determined that the struggling Episcopal Church in Santa Cruz should have its own permanent home: she deeded the site.

Eliza's wedding to Joseph Boston was the first recorded in the church register. It took place in May 1862, the same month the church had its first service. Earliest services had been held in various places—the Santa Cruz Courtroom, Temperance Hall on the Mission Street hill, an "old flea-infested schoolhouse recently vacated by the Methodists," the new Methodist Church, and private homes.

In 1864 the Episcopalians formed a new parish with Joseph Boston as secretary and the Rev. C. F. Loop as missionary rector. Joseph drew plans for the church building and the cornerstone was laid on June 29, 1864. The first (chilly) service in the new building (minus windows, altar and pulpit) was held January 8, 1865.

Ocean View Avenue

Ocean View was considered almost out in the country during the late 1800s when most of its large homes were constructed. The street was opened in 1870-71. It was "out," and afforded plenty of pasture for each family's carriage horses, yet it was close enough to the center of town for convenience.

Not to be overlooked were the magnificent views of Monterey Bay and the beach to the south, the city of Santa Cruz to the west, and the wooded mountains to the north.

Those were the days of large lots, circular driveways and carriage houses, indoor conservatories for the growing of rare flowers, and outdoors, garden gazebos and fountains.

Ladies served afternoon tea to callers (with the assistance of hired girls) and swished about their mansions in silk taffeta gowns over layers of finely embroidered petticoats.

Ocean View Avenue

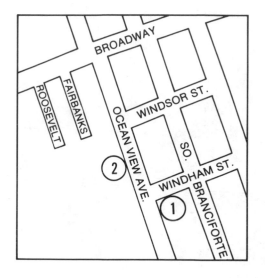

These houses were twins when built. Johnston House was "modernized" in the 1920s. Other imposing Victorians are also on this street.

(1) **Smith House—250 Ocean View Avenue.** One of the real showplaces of Santa Cruz, this beautiful Queen Anne with Eastlake touches was built in 1891.

(2) **Johnston House—317 Ocean View Avenue.** At the time it was built, in 1891, this house was described as ranking "among the first of the handsome homes of Santa Cruz."

– 1891 –
Smith House
250 Ocean View Avenue

This beautiful Queen Anne with Eastlake touches at the corner of Ocean View Avenue and Windham Street was built in 1891 for Captain W. W. Gray of Merced. The architect was LeBaron Olive. The house was acquired by Lucas F. Smith in 1894, to house his six children and to serve as his wife's social headquarters. Smith was an Indian fighter and a lawyer and in later years was presiding judge of Santa Cruz Superior Court. Southern-born Mrs. Smith, the former Della Gouldy, loved to entertain, and her Southern hospitality was a special feature of the Smith home.

Today the house is one of the showplaces of the town—thanks to a couple who bought it, restored it, and made it their home for about 10 years. Mr. and Mrs. Ed Perkins performed a labor of love on the old house, retaining the natural redwood woodwork and features such as the pressed metal paneling. The major change was in the kitchen, which was completely modernized although not structurally changed in any way—it is still a huge, old-fashioned looking kitchen. The Perkins' also added a powder room and several bathrooms.

Mr. and Mrs. Edward C. Sumpf became the owners of this lovely home in 1972.

– 1891 –
Johnston House
317 Ocean View Avenue

An article in the *Santa Cruz Surf* in November of 1891 said: "The Beautiful House Just Finished for A. M. Johnston . . . a leading merchant of this city. The symmetry and architectural beauty of the exterior, the comfort, elegance and completeness of the interior, and the magnificence of the views to be had from every window and porch, ranks this among the first of the handsome homes of Santa Cruz . . . "

The article goes on to describe various parts of the house. It had an entrance hall, front parlor, back parlor, dining room, a small library, a kitchen lauded as "one of the largest and most convenient rooms in the house with ample closets, a modern sink finished with a tiled front, and all the conveniences a thrifty housekeeper could wish for." A side porch contained a lavatory with "hot and cold water."

On the second floor were four large bedrooms, a bathroom, and a laundry chute to the basement laundry room. The second floor was reached by two stairways, one in front elegant with polished rail and woodwork, and a smaller one in back for the help. The attic extended over the entire house and was unfinished—except for the enchanting tower room!

It was described as "a delightful little room, which is all of glass, is cozily carpeted and furnished and the views from which 'cap the climax' of the lovely outdoor pictures which abound . . . "

The whole house was finished in natural redwood and lighted with electricity. A stable "corresponding in general design and finish to the house" was also built. The architect was LeBaron Olive.

Today this house is severe in its appearance, with all ornamental work removed sometime in the late '20s. Originally it was the twin of Smith House, across Ocean View Avenue from it.

Dr. and Mrs. Robert Matiasevich, the present owners, plan to restore the house, using the original photo as a guide.

Beach Hill Area

It's hard to imagine the earliest Santa Cruz days when Beach Hill was barren of houses and motels. The hill rose abruptly from the curving white sand beach where Costanoan Indians fished and hunted sea birds. The hill sloped only where the San Lorenzo River and Neary Lagoon had joined forces to carve a river outlet to Monterey Bay.

When the first Spanish settlers came to Mission Santa Cruz and a little later to Villa de Branciforte, sailing ships soon began dropping anchor offshore, to send small boats in closer to collect mission-grown vegetables and crops, cattle hides and bags of tallow. When the Yankees began to arrive, one early American settler found pieces of a wrecked boat on the beach and made a shelter for himself in which he lived for a few months.

Beach Hill began to attract home builders and boarding house resorts in the early 1860s. The famed Sea Beach Hotel grew out of one of those resorts. But the beach and hill really came into their own with the construction of the Neptune Baths in 1884. In 1903 the boardwalk and a more elaborate bath house were built, and in 1904 the Neptune Casino and Pleasure Pier were constructed. In 1911 the regal Casa del Rey Hotel was built and by then Beach Hill had its quota of lavish homes, some of which survive.

To see the best, walk up Cliff Street, then on top of the hill along Third Street.

Beach Hill Area

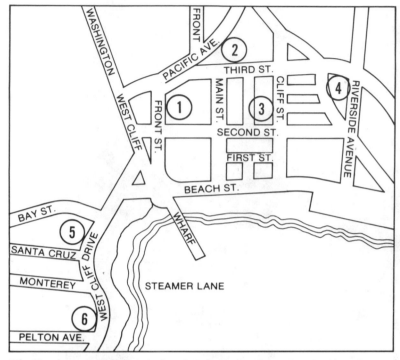

The Hotel stands like a sentinel at the entrance to Santa Cruz Beach and Wharf. Proceed on Third Street past the hotel to No. 2, and down to No. 4 at the foot of the hill. Come back up hill to Cliff, turn left and go down toward Casino and Casa Del Rey, passing No. 3. Proceed along the waterfront west to Municipal Wharf—time out for a shrimp cocktail—then go to West Cliff Drive to see No. 5. Proceed out Drive past No. 6 to see surfers at Steamer Lane, near Memorial Lighthouse.

(1) **Hotel McCray—80 Front Street.** The spacious lawns and extensive gardens are as impressive as the house they surround.

(2) **Golden Gate Villa—924 Third Street.** This house is an outstanding example of Queen Anne architecture.

(3) **Cliff Crest—407 Cliff Street.** This entire house was constructed of redwood. It was built in 1887, with an addition in 1904.

(4) **Rio Vista—611 Third Street.** Ten fine stained glass windows grace this lovely house.

(5) **Lynch House—170 W. Cliff Drive.** This is one of the finest examples of the Italianate style in Santa Cruz.

(6) **The Breakers—707 Pelton Avenue.** The view from this imposing house is a breathtaking one.

– **1867** –
Hotel McCray
(Sunshine Villa)
Beach Hill

It hasn't been a hotel for some years, but Hotel McCray still bears that name above its main entrance. The old structure, with mansard roof and half-timbering, goes back to a far more elegant past when there were iron deer "grazing" on the spacious lawns and a bronze fountain from the Orient splashing rainbow drops.

The original part of the building in the rear was built in 1867 for Dr. Francis M. Kittredge, who came to California in 1849. The main building was constructed in 1883 with John Williams as architect.

In 1890 the socialite James P. Smiths arrived in Santa Cruz and purchased the Villa and grounds for about $24,000. They added the deer and fountain, and imported plants and trees from many parts of the world for their extensive gardens. Mrs. Smith masterminded the famed Santa Cruz Venetian Water Carnival of 1895 (with the help of her husband's pocketbook). The San Lorenzo River was dammed for the event, forming a lake which was lit with strings of electric lights at night. The Smiths' daughter was crowned Queen and led the water parade on an elaborate barge. The Smiths lived at the Villa and entertained lavishly until 1920. The structure passed through many hands and became, for a time, a hotel.

– 1891 –
Golden Gate Villa
(Palaise Monte Carlo)
924 Third Street

Perhaps the finest example in Santa Cruz of Queen Anne style, this elegant house was built in 1891 by Major Frank W. McLaughlin. The architect was T. J. Welch. Originally the third floor tower, or belvedere, was open, with arched openings and columns. It was enclosed in recent years, and that is the most noticeable change that has been made.

The house cost about $20,000 to build, even in those days. It contains many fine stained glass windows, elephant hide on walls of one room, an onyx fireplace and some gold-plated lighting fixtures. The original decorating was done by Fraser and Keefe of San Francisco. The house has six chimneys and 22 rooms. Windows in some rooms depict fruits, flowers, and musical instruments.

Major McLaughlin had had a fabulous career, including a connection with the Edison Phonograph Company (he was a close friend of Thomas Edison), the building of a nine-mile tunnel for the Big Bend Project, and a 30-mile flume for the Miocene Hydraulic Mine. These and other endeavors brought him fame and fortune back East, before he came west and failed in an ill-conceived project to divert and dam the Feather River. He came to Santa Cruz to live in his big house, but after his wife died a few years later, he grieved and brooded, and finally planned the murder of his stepdaughter, Agnes, and suicide, to happen on the second anniversary of his wife's death. He wrote 15 farewell letters a few months before, and when the fateful day came, he put a revolver to the temple of the sleeping Agnes, and then drank cyanide.

On a happier note, the beautiful and elegant house became the property, in 1967, of a woman who had fallen in love with it when she was a small girl. Patricia Sambuck Wilkinson has spent years in a labor of love, restoring, cleaning, painting, and searching for the right pieces of furniture for the house. Palais Monte Carlo—or Patty's Palace, as it is now sometimes called, is an apartment house and she lives in one of them. The house has been awarded the California Heritage Council's Certificate of Recognition.

– 1887 –
Cliff Crest
407 Cliff Street

Strong Queen Anne influence is seen in the design of Cliff-Crest, which was constructed in 1887 for $1,500 for Mrs. A. E. Perkins. Daniel Damkroger was the architect. The solarium and belvedere were added in 1903-04.

William and Jennie Jeter purchased Cliff-Crest in the 1890s. Jeter served as Lieutenant-Governor of the State of California from 1895 to 1899, but the single accomplishment for which he is best remembered is the magnificent stand of redwoods near Felton. The Jeters were early-day ecologists before that word had been coined. He organized the Big Trees Company from his death bed in a Santa Cruz hospital, in order to save a portion of the redwoods that are today called Henry Cowell Redwoods State Park.

The home includes a drawing room, living room, dining room, solarium, kitchen, three bedrooms, baths and belvedere. There are fireplaces in the dining and living rooms. The solarium contains stained glass that is truly unusual, echoing the colors and feeling of Gauguin paintings. In the dining room there are leaded glass doors on the china cabinet. A curved handrail on the staircase was added by the Jeters.

The entire house is constructed of redwood, with a total square footage of about 3,300 feet.

The Jeters were friends of John McLaren, the land-scape designer of Golden Gate Park in San Francisco. His influence is seen in the gardens, which include many unusual plantings. Still thriving after more than 50 years are Belgian laurel, Japanese camellia, a giant mattress vine, several unusual fuschias, two gingko trees, a deep purple tulip tree, and two palm trees.

– 1890 –
Rio Vista
611 Third Street

"View of the River" is an appropriate title for this Stick and Eastlake house which contains ten very fine stained glass windows.

It was built in 1890 for a Mrs. M. Barfield, with LeBaron Olive as the architect.

This house, with its magnificent view of the San Lorenzo River and the town of Santa Cruz with its mountain backdrop, is today painted in its original colors of light and dark green.

– 1877 –
Lynch House
170 West Cliff Drive

Originally one of the finest examples of the Italianate style in Santa Cruz, Lynch House was built for a builder, Sedgwick Lynch.

It cost $12,000 to construct in 1877. John Morrow was the architect.

Lynch arrived in California from Pennsylvania in 1849 after crossing the Isthmus of Panama. For a time he worked as an oiler on a Sacramento River steamer, before going to the gold mines in 1850. He struck a rich vein of ore and in 1851 was back in San Francisco, where he served on the Vigilance Committee.

However, Lynch's true gold strike was his trade. He became a general contractor and prospered, constructing buildings in many parts of California. When he came to Santa Cruz to enjoy his fortune, he wanted a fine home near Monterey Bay. This was it.

– 1887 –
The Breakers
707 Pelton

The Breakers rises in majestic simplicity on the corner of Pelton and West Cliff Drive, little changed from the day it was completed in 1887. Its windows are large and many, with a breathtaking sweep to the east of

Monterey Bay, Santa Cruz City, the Municipal Wharf and waterfront. The house is built of redwood, as are most of Santa Cruz's fine old homes. Its trim is simple, spool and spindle in the eaves above the windows, and many small spindles around the top of the porches. The siding is shiplap, and the style is Eastlake, done with great restraint.

The house was built for C. C. Wheeler, who sold it after one year to a Methodist Bishop, Henry Warren. The Warrens first called it "Epworth by the Sea" for the English birthplace of John Wesley, founder of Methodism. Later the name was changed to "The Breakers," more in keeping with its enchanting view of Monterey Bay.

Bishop and Mrs. Warren came to Santa Cruz from Colorado, where Mrs. Warren owned extensive ranch holdings and was known as the "Cattle Queen." She had formerly been married to a member of the wealthy Iliff family of Denver, and her gifts established the Iliff School of Theology there.

Eventually the Warrens bought an entire block facing the Bay. It was bounded by West Cliff Drive, Santa Cruz Avenue, Gharkey Street, and Lighthouse Avenue.

For years, members of the Warren and Iliff families spent vacations at "The Breakers." The last member of the family to live there was a daughter, Edna Iliff Briggs. She died in San Francisco in 1951 and as part of her estate, "The Breakers" was sold. Today it is an apartment house, appropriately named "The Breakers Apartments."

Other areas best visited by auto trips

– 1912 –
Calreta Court
260 High Street

This impressive Mission Revival apartment house was built in 1912 with William Bray as architect. It was called Piedmont Court, and when built was described as "Moorish in design, with an elaborate interior court with fountain." Especially notable are its twin towers and twin espadanas, which are decorated with variations of the quatrefoil.

Santa Cruzans sat up and took notice when they heard that a 50-room apartment house was to be built. In a day when most homes were heated with wood fires and many people were still pumping water by hand, it was understandable that a building with steam heat, electricity, and hot and cold running water through-out would be impressive.

Work began in August 1912, and no expense was spared in creating the finest apartment house in town. John Church was construction superintendent, George Cardiff supplied cement, and T. F. Costella was in charge of all cement work.

The man with all the fancy ideas and the money to carry them out was a wealthy native of Sonora, Mexico, Don Pedro Chisem. He "discovered" Santa Cruz about 144 years after the first Spanish explorers had marched through, but, as with each new "discoverer," he believed that he had found a truly unique place. He was impressed with the climate, the beauty of the town, and the financial possibilities. He had a wallet bulging with Mexican banknotes, money which came from his interests in silver mines.

But before the stately Piedmont Court was finished, political upheavals in Mexico caused Don Pedro's silver flood to dwindle to virtually nothing, and his ventures in Santa Cruz had to come to an end. The apartment house was completed with money put up by Frank G. Wilson and Bruce Sharpe, local businessmen.

In 1952 the handsome building was purchased by the California Retired Teachers Association. They gave it the name "Calreta Court" and today Don Pedro's dream is home to a group of retired educators.

– 1906 –
Dake House
410 High Street

So tall are the trees and shrubs around this house that it can hardly be seen from High Street, which is directly below it at a much lower level. The house is located on a large lot against the hill, above the street, and is reached by a long flight of steps which cut up through the fine limestone wall that fronts the property. A winding driveway curves up behind the house to the garage.

The house was originally a handsome Colonial Revival. It has been slightly changed in appearance in recent years, with the addition of enclosed areas on the front porch, which was open when built. The main entry is directly beneath the second floor balcony railing. Every window on this south side of the house has a sweeping view of Santa Cruz and Monterey Bay—if the shrubs are trimmed! The house is redwood with a full concrete basement and full attic—it is really four stories.

This home was constructed in 1906 by Mr. and Mrs. Lawrence J. Dake. It remained in the Dake family as the home of the elder son, Clarence, until 1933. It was a comfortable and large home in a day when large houses were the general rule. The front stair led up from an entry hall that was a room in itself with fireplace and windows overlooking the city. A back stair served for the hired help and took off from the back hall which ran the length of the house. The dining room and entry hall fireplaces were corner ones; the large living room had a larger fireplace on its west wall. There were five big bedrooms on the second floor, all but one with glorious views out over the city and bay.

– c. 1850 –
Cowell House
1001 High Street

In 1964, before he died, George Cardiff, who worked for the Cowell family for many years, estimated that the original part of the Cowell Ranch home at Santa Cruz was from 110 to 112 years old. The oldest part of the house contains the kitchen with its huge fireplace, reminiscent of New England homes where a black iron pot of beans or stew was always bubbling over the fire. In later years, rooms were added onto what is the front of the house today, probably by the Cowells, who lived there from 1865 to 1897. The house is simple in style, resembling the California adobe to a degree, with redwood siding and slender square posts holding its front porch roof.

The original portion of the house was built by Albion P. Jordan, pioneer lime industrialist who came to the county in 1853. He established a partnership with Isaac E. Davis, and in 1865 sold his share and his home to Henry Cowell.

Henry Cowell and his wife, Alice, had five children: Isabella, Ernest, Samuel H., Helen and Agnes. Samuel H. was known as Harry, and it was he who spent the most time at the family's Santa Cruz ranch. Henry Cowell was a despotic patriarch who ruled the lives of his children and decreed that they were not to marry; suitors could only be after their money. One son, Ernest, rebelled and was married without parental blessings. He was ostracized, but later reinstated when he broke with his wife. He was the Cowell who left $250,000 to the University of California for construction of Cowell Infirmary on the Berkeley campus.

In 1897 the Cowells moved from Santa Cruz to San Francisco. Six years later Henry Cowell died, and in the same year the youngest daughter, Agnes, was killed on the Santa Cruz ranch. She had come down to spend a day or so, and went out to pick wild flowers; it was May and they were blooming in the meadows. She took a horse and buggy—a high-spirited horse she had been warned against using. She and the Cowell housekeeper set out across the fields, a buggy wheel struck a rock, the horse bolted and Agnes was thrown from the buggy. She died of a broken neck.

As a result of the accident, Isabella never set foot in Santa Cruz again. She and the other sister, Helen, lived as recluses on one of the family estates at Atherton. When Helen died in 1932, Isabella moved out and had a bulldozer come in and flatten their home. She left it that way—smashed in collapsed ruins, and went to San Francisco to live with her brother Harry.

– c. 1880 –
The Cookhouse
U.C.S.C. Campus

The Cowell Ranch Cookhouse always was red, although all the other buildings on the ranch were whitewashed.

The building was used as a cookhouse from the 1880s to the early 1950s. It was built into a hillside and has a foundation of stone and concrete; the structure itself is redwood lumber. Equipment in the place consisted of an old wood-burning stove, a sink, a few tables and chairs, and coal oil lamps. There was no electricity until after 1949. A small screened cabin at one end was the meat cooler, and a pigsty in front was the garbage disposal.

The Cookhouse stands on the site of the earliest quarry on the Cowell property, which was first mined for limestone by Isaac Davis and Albion P. Jordan. Henry Cowell bought Jordan's limestone interests in 1865 and Davis's portion in 1888. The ranch covered approximately 2,000 acres of pasture dotted with huge old oak trees and redwood forests.

The future of the Cookhouse was assured on March 17, 1961, when the Regents of the University of California announced their decision to found a new branch of the University on the Cowell Ranch at Santa Cruz. In January 1965, Chancellor Dean E. McHenry moved into his office in the renovated Cookhouse, where the main conservation piece was the old wood cook stove, which has been there ever since. The building and the "stove office" are now used by the University Security and Parking Departments.

– c. 1900 –
The Newer Baldwin House
445 Locust Street

A cousin of Levi Baldwin, F. D. Baldwin, built this home after the turn of the century, but it reflects an earlier era with its rounded cupola, bow windows and carriage house in the backyard. In the soft bitumen paving of the driveway, one can yet see the prints of horses' hooves, left over from carriage days.

In the backyard, next to the carriage house, stands the original Baldwin home, which was built in the 1860s. It originally stood at the front of the property, but was moved back to make way for the new, more elaborate house, a modified Queen Anne.

F. D. Baldwin, like his cousin Levi, was born in Massachusetts and went into dairying when he came to California. He was also a teacher, a Santa Cruz County Supervisor for two terms, chairman of the County Republican Central Committee, and a director of the City Bank of Santa Cruz and the City Savings Bank. He helped to frame the Santa Cruz City Charter, and was an active and interested citizen all his life—which lasted past his 96th birthday.

– c. 1880 –
Baldwin House
425 Locust Street

There is something faintly Gothic about this plain little house at 425 Locust Street. Perhaps "Carpenter Gothic" would be a better term. Yet its simple lines have worn well through the years since it was built, in about 1880. It is of redwood, shiplap siding, with pierced posts holding its porch roof.

The house was built by Harrison Terry, who sold it to Levi Baldwin in 1898. Ever since then some member of the Baldwin family has lived here. The current owner and resident is Miss Ruth Baldwin.

This little pioneer frame house has sheltered a passing parade of weddings, births, funerals, family get-togethers, and just plain everyday living. The early-day Baldwin family was a friendly tangle of "kissing cousins." The first to come west was Levi, who had been a prosperous farmer in Massachusetts until business reverses wiped him out. He was a generous man and had endorsed mortgages for friends, then had to mortgage his own home to meet the notes when they fell due.

In 1858 Levi and his wife came to California via the Isthmus of Panama, settling first in Marin County where he operated a dairy. In 1872 he moved to Santa Cruz to start another dairy, which became famous for its butter. He developed the business from his original purchase of 157 acres and 23 cows to 1,700 acres and 400 cows. In Santa Cruz he regained the wealth and prestige he had lost in the East. He became president of Santa Cruz County Bank in the 1890s, and before that had served as a county supervisor.

When Levi died, the little house on Locust Street went to his daughter, May. In 1906 May deeded the property to Carrie Baldwin, the wife of a cousin. When Carrie died in 1953, the house passed to her daughter, Ruth, who lives there still, with many happy and colorful memories.

– c. 1886 –
Weeks House
724 California Street

This magnificent structure with its cupolas, tower, gables, scrolls, flutings, knobs and swirls was built about 1886 for Thomas Jefferson Weeks. One of Santa Cruz's truly important Eastlake houses, with touches of Queen Anne, it cost $9,000—a princely sum for a home in those days.

One report has it that LeBaron Oliver was the architect; another states that Daniel Damkroger designed the elaborate home.

Complete with brackets, a finial on its tower and quatrefoil trim on porches, Weeks House is something to see, indeed. Arched windows are finished with decorated trim. Siding is redwood shiplap. Porch pillars are elaborately turned and embellished.

The house originally stood on Walnut Avenue hill, commanding a magnificent panoramic view of Monterey Bay and the Santa Cruz beach, where Weeks had lived in a shack when he first arrived in California. It was moved to its present location in 1913, to make way for Santa Cruz High School.

The interior of this house is as fascinating as its ornate exterior, with a hallway paneled with pressed leather and one fireplace inlaid with redwood burl.

Acclaimed at the time it was built as "one of the most commodious and attractive [homes] in the entire county," today the Weeks House is one of a handful of Santa Cruz's truly spectacular Victorians. Through the years it has had a number of owners. The current ones are Mr. and Mrs. Robert Page, who treasure every detail.

Log Cabin Home, Laurel St.

– 1910 –
Babbling Brook
1025 Laurel Street

On Laurel Street in Santa Cruz, just midway on the
hill, is an old log cabin—real logs, no fake about it. It
was built with whole redwood logs, the bark left on, in
1909-10. Later the house was embellished with decora-
tive iron work, over the windows and inside, made by
Otar the Lampmaker of Santa Cruz, who had his studio
on Pacific Avenue.

The log house is reminiscent of the Swiss chalet style, with a balcony from the second story portion. The upper area of the second story is redwood shingles. A stream of water comes shooting out of the hill at its feet, wanders through the garden below the cabin, and disappears again, to lose itself in Neary Lagoon.

The log house is named Babbling Brook. It was built by Mr. and Mrs. Charlie Place, touring actors who decided they wanted to settle down in Santa Cruz. However, after a short time the lure of the footlights got to them again, and they sold the house and left to go on tour.

For years the place was known as the Log Cabin. At one time it belonged to Mr. and Mrs. Peter Rovnianek. He was Consul from Slovakia to the United States. They enlarged the cabin a bit and developed gardens.

Later owners were Mr. and Mrs. Charles Chandler. He was a San Francisco attorney and she was a countess—by wishful thinking, some still say. A native of Austria, she is said to have received her title through a former marriage to the late Count Nikolai of Austria. Whether or not she had a right to the title, she claimed it and was always—but *always*—addressed as Madame Countess.

The Chandlers sold the log cabin to Mr. and Mrs. Lloyd Wright, who operated a restaurant in it, then leased it out to other restaurateurs.

In 1973 Frances McReynolds Smith got it. "Got it" is the correct term—"I had to have it," she says with a smile. A lecturer at the University of California at Santa Cruz, Mrs. Smith rescued much of the ornamental iron work and now makes her home in the log house.

– c. 1870 –
Rydell House
201 Maple Street

In the last few years a startling transformation has taken place at 201 Maple Street—corner of Maple and Cedar Streets. A rather nondescript old stick style house has evolved from ugly duckling into near-swan. Responsible for the change is Roy Rydell, Santa Cruz landscape architect who designed the Pacific Garden mall landscaping for the city. He has also co-authored a book on landscape gardening published by Sunset.

The house at 201 Maple evolved out of a plain farmhouse built there about 1869-70. It is located on what was once the Rodriguez Tract, then became the property of Frederick A. Hihn, and was later sold to a Mrs. McAlmond. In 1869 she sold it back to Mr. Hihn and it isn't clear whether or not the house was standing there at that time. The land and the house eventually became the property of Charles M. Collins of the Collins and Maxwell Grocery firm. Collins doubled the size of the original house and hired an architect to bestow upon it what style it has ever possessed. He was Daniel A. Damkroger, the architect who designed Weeks House and several other notable structures in Santa Cruz.

Work started in October 1887 and by December was almost complete. The *Santa Cruz Surf* proclaimed the remodeled house "an ornament to the corner." Today, after many years as a rooming house, it is an ornament again, thanks to landscaping, a coat of dark paint, and an attractive picket fence. There are two apartments upstairs and Mr. Rydell's office is downstairs. The house serves as a subtle reminder that "stick" and "carpenter Gothic" houses were originally intended to blend into foliage which softened their effect. They were often painted tan or green, to enhance this blending, and their wood trim, "board nailed on top of board," often copied Gothic stone traceries.

– c. 1850 –
Blackburn House
152 Center Street

Built in the 1850s by Judge William Blackburn, for whom Blackburn Gulch and Blackburn Street were named, this house is a Greek Revival, with plain boxed cornices and shiplap siding. It is best viewed from the junction of Cedar and Sycamore Streets.

William Blackburn was known as a "character"—and a man not to be fooled with. He came to Alta California in 1845. In 1846 he joined the California Bear Flag Battalion under Captain John C. Fremont. After the excitement of trying to capture Alta California for the United States, Blackburn came back to settle in Santa Cruz. He opened a hotel and store on Holy Cross Plaza, which was the center of town in those days. His two-story adobe building was called the Eagle Hotel.

Blackburn was appointed Alcalde of Santa Cruz, and later became Justice of the Peace under Territorial Government.

In 1859, when he was 45 years old, the Judge married Harriet Mead. The wedding took place in the home of Harriet's brother-in-law and sister, Dr. and Mrs. J. C. Kittredge. It stood at the tip of Beach Hill and today is known as Hotel McCray.

By the 1860s the Judge was recognized as the city's richest citizen, but his wealth did not prevent tragedy. His only child, a two-year-old son, died in 1864, and he himself died three years later.

– 1860 –
Hagemann House
105 Mentel Avenue

One of the largest single-dwelling properties remaining in the City of Santa Cruz, this unusual house with its twin towers cannot be viewed from the street. It is approached by way of a long, winding driveway through a grove of eucalyptus and cypress trees. The property includes about seven and one-third acres, with wild azalea thickets and ferns in a ravine, coveys of quail, raccoons and oppossums—a lively population of small creatures who can manage to survive with city life surrounding them. To the south, a short walk away over meadow and grassy pastureland, is Santa Cruz Small Crafts Harbor.

This structure is often referred to as a "cottage," but what it might lack in size, it more than makes up in elaborate wood and metal trim, and towers—two of them! The house has been labeled Italianate Victorian, but the towers give it an Oriental, almost Persian or Moorish feeling, which is enhanced by the lacy woodwork. Inside, the house is little changed. The original wallpapers are intact in the main rooms and the entry hall. Mr. and Mrs. Charles H. Gunn, the present owners, have furnished the house with their own collection of beautiful antiques as well as Mrs. Gunn's sculpture (she is a scupltress of note) and the fine metal sculpture of her partner, John Sillstrop. Even the shirred white silk curtains at the living room windows are replicas of those that hung there when the Hagemanns were in residence, as seen in a photograph of the time, now in the Gunns' possession. In addition to two "parlors," master bedroom, dining room and kitchen downstairs, the house has four bedrooms upstairs.

The house was built in the 1860s as a farm house of much simpler design. In 1885 the front rooms and towers were added, with architect Emil John directing the work. A beautiful fence also was constructed and yet survives. The original owner was Frederick Hagemann, an associate of Claus Spreckels. He raised hogs, cattle, wheat, and chickens, and also built the Hagemann Hotel on Pacific Avenue. When he first came to live on his Live Oak Ranch, it was considered "way out in the country." Today the 110 acres he owned have shrunk to less than eight, and the city limits have crept out to enfold the property with its "blue gum forest" and hidden ravine.

– 1870 –
The Little White Church
Soquel

In 1870 a ship's carpenter from Maine, S. A. Hall, began the task of building a suitable house of worship for Soquel Congregationalists, who had been meeting for four years in a blacksmith shop.

Hall envisioned a New England-type church, like the ones in Maine where he grew up. He drew plans, perhaps working on a sheet of coarse brown paper with a stubby pencil. Then he headed the volunteer work crews who put up the church. The lot on which it was built was a gift from Joshua Parrish, Soquel pioneer. At that time land around Soquel was valued at $14.22 per acre. Soquel families—a handful of them—raised the $2,700 the church cost. It was dedicated August 7, 1870. The spire was 60 feet tall; the 1,000 pound bell was placed in it in 1877 by the Rev. A. C. Duncan.

Over the years some changes were necessary. In 1893 the building was moved 20 feet and a choir alcove was added. In 1903 the kerosene lamps were replaced with a carbide lighting plant. In 1905 the social hall was built and a year later $76 was spent for a shed to protect the horses that drew the buggies and wagons of churchgoers.

In 1925 the church starred as the background for a movie, *Johnstown Flood*, in which Janet Gaynor was featured as the tragic bride who was swept away during her wedding ceremony.

In 1943 the chancel was rebuilt. A set of 21 chimes was installed in 1954. In 1964 the church fathers realized that more extensive work was needed on the sanctuary. The steeple spire was in danger of collapsing due to rot and termites. New flooring was necessary; also wiring and a foundation under the entire structure. Everybody got busy to raise the needed $25,000. There were church suppers, rummage sales, and many donations. The work was done, with a final touch of a coat of fresh white paint.

A few months later a fire broke out in the steeple, and the entire town of Soquel, agnostics and churchgoers alike, waited anxiously while it was brought under control.

– c. 1870 –
The Bay View Hotel
Aptos

The Bay View Hotel in Aptos was built about 1870 by Jose Arano, a French immigrant who married the youngest daughter of Don Rafael Castro, who owned the 6,680-acre Rancho Aptos. It is Italianate with French mansard roof, a style popular in the 1860s to 1880s. It was originally two stories high, and it housed Arano's grocery store and the Aptos Post Office for a time. It is said that when the hotel was under construction, Arano personally inspected every bit of lumber that went into it. He also selected every stick of furniture, most of which is there today. The four handsome marble fireplaces on the main floor are originals. The third floor was added in 1883.

For more than 40 years the Bay View was a popular watering place for wealthy and prominent people. Its guests included Lillian Russell and King Kalakaua of Hawaii at various times. When Claus Spreckels, the sugar beet king, bought a large part of Rancho Aptos, he brought many famous visitors to the Bay View.

The hotel was a busy place when the Loma Prieta Lumber Company was running full blast. F. A. Hihn's Valencia Mill also shipped from Aptos, and the busiest years were 1880 to 1900. However, the great redwood trees in the hills were finally logged out, railroad activity was curtailed, and shortly before World War I the hotel closed.

In 1944 Fred W. Toney and his wife, Elma, bought the old building. A service wing had burned in 1929 but the main structure was intact. In spite of warnings by professional house movers that it couldn't be done, Toney and a crew of Aptos men placed timbers and rollers beneath the building and moved it about 100 feet to its present location. It formerly stood at the corner of Trout Gulch Road, nearer the railroad tracks.

Fred and Elma ran the Bay View as a hotel and eating place until 1972. They now lease it out to Frank Leal and Pete Marchese, who operate it as a hotel, restaurant and bar.

– 1926 –
Howden's Castle
Ben Lomond

Robert Howden's Ben Lomond home was his castle, and his stone castle was his home.

He called himself an "everyday Scotsman," but his burning desire was to live in a castle. He did. He built it himself. He selected a beautiful bend on the San

Lorenzo River in Ben Lomond, and there, in the early 1920s, with local hired help, he built his castle. He patterned it after castles he remembered from his boyhood days in Scotland.

The castle went together slowly. Every stone was hand-picked and hand set. Howden's regular home and business were located in Oakland, where he operated a tile factory, but his heart was in the "highlands" of Ben Lomond.

The castle was completed in 1926, with only three rooms. Howden had spent his early life in Scotland as a stone carver, and he used his talent to etch the panes of the glass windows in his castle. They depict Scottich scenes and the poems of Sir Walter Scott and Robert Burns.

Howden kept his castle until 1937, when he sold it to Dr. and Mrs. Norman Sullivan of Santa Cruz, who enlarged it and modernized a bit. Since then it has changed hands four times and each new owner has added to its comfort and charm without changing the basic appearance. Today it contains about 15 rooms, some of them quite small, according to Mrs. Ivy Lee Weatherly, who owns it and lives there with her flock of 12 cats. She opens the castle for tours on Saturdays, Sundays and holidays.

Robert Howden once wrote these lines: "Ben Lomond, nestling 'mong the heights, Above fair Santa Cruz, Your peaceful quiet my soul delights, Your charm awakes my muse . . . "